Authentic
Leadership

HBR EMOTIONAL INTELLIGENCE SERIES

HBR Emotional Intelligence Series

How to be human at work

The HBR Emotional Intelligence Series features smart, essential reading on the human side of professional life from the pages of *Harvard Business Review*.

Authentic Leadership

Empathy

Happiness

Influence and Persuasion

Mindfulness

Resilience

Other books on emotional intelligence from *Harvard Business Review*:

HBR's 10 Must Reads on Emotional Intelligence

HBR Guide to Emotional Intelligence

Authentic Leadership

HBR EMOTIONAL INTELLIGENCE SERIES

Harvard Business Review Press

Boston, Massachusetts

HBR Press Quantity Sales Discounts

Harvard Business Review Press titles are available at significant quantity discounts when purchased in bulk for client gifts, sales promotions, and premiums. Special editions, including books with corporate logos, customized covers, and letters from the company or CEO printed in the front matter, as well as excerpts of existing books, can also be created in large quantities for special needs.

For details and discount information for both print and ebook formats, contact booksales@harvardbusiness.org, tel. 800-988-0886, or www.hbr.org/bulksales.

Copyright 2018 Harvard Business School Publishing Corporation
All rights reserved
Printed in the United States of America

10 9 8 7 6 5 4 3 2

No part of this publication may be reproduced, stored in or introduced into a retrieval system, or transmitted, in any form, or by any means (electronic, mechanical, photocopying, recording, or otherwise), without the prior permission of the publisher. Requests for permission should be directed to permissions@hbsp.harvard.edu, or mailed to Permissions, Harvard Business School Publishing, 60 Harvard Way, Boston, Massachusetts 02163.

The web addresses referenced in this book were live and correct at the time of the book's publication but may be subject to change.

Library of Congress Cataloging-in-Publication Data

Title: Authentic leadership.
Other titles: HBR emotional intelligence series.
Description: Boston, Massachusetts : Harvard Business Review Press, [2017] | Series: HBR emotional intelligence series | Includes index.
Identifiers: LCCN 2017027307 | ISBN 9781633693913 (pbk. : alk. paper)
Subjects: LCSH: Leadership—Psychological aspects. | Self-consciousness (Awareness) | Authenticity (Philosophy) | Corporate culture.
Classification: LCC HD57.7 .A8496 2017 | DDC 658.4/092—dc23 LC record available at https://lccn.loc.gov/2017027307

The paper used in this publication meets the requirements of the American National Standard for Permanence of Paper for Publications and Documents in Libraries and Archives Z39.48-1992.

ISBN: 978-1-63369-391-3
eISBN: 978-1-63369-329-0

Contents

Contents

Authentic
Leadership

HBR EMOTIONAL INTELLIGENCE SERIES

1

Discovering Your Authentic Leadership

By Bill George, Peter Sims, Andrew N. McLean, and Diana Mayer

During the past 50 years, leadership scholars have conducted more than 1,000 studies in an attempt to determine the definitive styles, characteristics, or personality traits of great leaders. None of these studies has produced a clear profile of the ideal leader. Thank goodness. If scholars had produced a cookie-cutter leadership style, individuals would be forever trying to imitate it. They would make themselves into personae, not people, and others would see through them immediately.

No one can be authentic by trying to imitate someone else. You can learn from others' experiences, but there is no way you can be successful when you are trying to be like them. People trust you when you are genuine and authentic, not a replica of someone else. Amgen CEO and president Kevin Sharer, who gained priceless experience working as Jack Welch's assistant in the 1980s, saw the downside of GE's cult of personality in those days. "Everyone wanted to be like Jack," he explains. "Leadership has many voices. You need to be who you are, not try to emulate somebody else."

Over the past five years, people have developed a deep distrust of leaders. It is increasingly evident that we need a new kind of business leader in the 21st century. In 2003, Bill George's book, *Authentic Leadership: Rediscovering the Secrets to Creating Lasting Value*, challenged a new generation to lead authentically. Authentic leaders demonstrate a passion for their purpose, practice their values consistently, and lead with their hearts as well as their heads. They establish long-term, meaningful relationships and have the self-discipline to get results. They know who they are.

Many readers of *Authentic Leadership*, including several CEOs, indicated that they had a tremendous desire to become authentic leaders and wanted to know how. As a result, our research team set out to answer the question, "How can people become and remain authentic leaders?" We interviewed 125 leaders to learn how they developed their leadership abilities. These interviews constitute the largest in-depth study of leadership development ever undertaken. Our interviewees discussed openly and honestly how they realized their potential and candidly shared their life stories, personal struggles, failures, and triumphs.

The people we talked with ranged in age from 23 to 93, with no fewer than 15 per decade. They were chosen based on their reputations for authenticity and effectiveness as leaders, as well as our personal knowledge of them. We also solicited recommendations from other leaders and academics. The resulting group includes women and men from a diverse array of racial, religious, and socioeconomic backgrounds and nationalities. Half of them are CEOs, and the other half comprises a range of profit and nonprofit leaders, midcareer leaders, and young leaders just starting on their journeys.

After interviewing these individuals, we believe we understand why more than 1,000 studies have not produced a profile of an ideal leader. Analyzing 3,000 pages of transcripts, our team was startled to see that these people did not identify any universal characteristics, traits, skills, or styles that led to their success. Rather, their leadership emerged from their life stories. Consciously and subconsciously, they were constantly testing themselves through real-world experiences and reframing their life stories to understand who they were at their core. In doing so, they discovered the purpose of their leadership and learned that being authentic made them more effective.

These findings are extremely encouraging: You do not have to be born with specific characteristics or traits of a leader. You do not have to wait for a tap on the shoulder. You do not have to be at the top of your organization. Instead, you can discover your potential right now. As one of our interviewees, Young & Rubicam chairman and CEO Ann Fudge, said, "All of us have the spark of leadership in us, whether it is in business, in government, or as a nonprofit volunteer. The challenge is to understand ourselves well enough to discover where we can use our leadership gifts to serve others."

Discovering your authentic leadership requires a commitment to developing yourself. Like musicians and athletes, you must devote yourself to a lifetime of realizing your potential. Most people Kroger CEO David Dillon has seen become good leaders were self-taught. Dillon said, "The advice I give to individuals in our company is not to expect the company to hand you a development plan. You need to take responsibility for developing yourself."

In the following pages, we draw upon lessons from our interviews to describe how people become authentic leaders. First and most important, they frame their life stories in ways that allow them to see themselves not as passive observers of their lives but rather as individuals who can develop self-awareness from their experiences. Authentic leaders act on that awareness by practicing their values and principles, sometimes at substantial risk to themselves. They are careful to balance their motivations so that they are driven by these inner values as much as by a desire for external rewards or recognition. Authentic leaders also keep a strong support team around them, ensuring that they live integrated, grounded lives.

Learning from your life story

The journey to authentic leadership begins with understanding the story of your life. Your life story provides the context for your experiences, and through it, you can find the inspiration to make an impact in the world. As the novelist John Barth once wrote, "The story of your life is not your life. It is your story." In other words, it is your personal narrative that matters, not the mere facts of your life. Your life narrative is like a permanent recording playing in your head. Over and over, you replay the events and personal interactions that are important to your life, attempting to make sense of them to find your place in the world.

While the life stories of authentic leaders cover the full spectrum of experiences—including the positive impact of parents, athletic coaches, teachers, and mentors—many leaders reported that their motivation came from a difficult experience in their lives. They described the transformative effects of the loss of a job; personal illness; the untimely death of a close friend or relative; and feelings of being excluded, discriminated against, and rejected by peers. Rather than seeing themselves as victims, though, authentic leaders used these formative experiences to give meaning to their lives. They reframed these events to rise above their challenges and to discover their passion to lead.

Let's focus now on one leader in particular, Novartis chairman and CEO Daniel Vasella, whose life story was one of the most difficult of all the people we interviewed. He emerged from extreme challenges in his youth to reach the pinnacle of the global pharmaceutical industry, a trajectory that illustrates the trials many leaders have to go through on their journeys to authentic leadership.

Vasella was born in 1953 to a modest family in Fribourg, Switzerland. His early years were filled with medical problems that stoked his passion to become a physician. His first recollections were of a hospital where he was admitted at age four when he suffered from food poisoning. Falling ill with asthma at age five, he was sent alone to the mountains of eastern Switzerland for two summers. He found the four-month separations from his parents especially difficult because his caretaker had an alcohol problem and was unresponsive to his needs.

At age eight, Vasella had tuberculosis, followed by meningitis, and was sent to a sanatorium for a year. Lonely and homesick, he suffered a great deal that year, as his parents rarely visited him. He still remembers the pain and fear when the nurses held him down during the lumbar punctures so that he would not move. One day, a new physician arrived and took time to explain each step of the procedure. Vasella asked the doctor if he could hold a nurse's hand rather than being held down. "The amazing thing is that this time the procedure didn't hurt," Vasella recalls. "Afterward, the doctor asked me, 'How was that?' I reached up and gave him a big hug. These human gestures of forgiveness, caring, and compassion made a deep impression on me and on the kind of person I wanted to become."

Throughout his early years, Vasella's life continued to be unsettled. When he was 10, his 18-year-old sister passed away after suffering from cancer for two years. Three years later, his father died in surgery. To support the family, his mother went to work in a distant town and came home only once every three weeks. Left to himself, he and his friends held beer parties and got into frequent fights. This lasted for three years until he met his first girlfriend, whose affection changed his life.

At 20, Vasella entered medical school, later graduating with honors. During medical school, he sought out psychotherapy so he could come to terms with his early experiences and not feel like a victim. Through analysis, he reframed his life story and realized that he wanted to help a wider range of people than he could as an individual practitioner. Upon completion of his residency, he applied to become chief physician at the University of Zurich; however, the search committee considered him too young for the position.

Disappointed but not surprised, Vasella decided to use his abilities to increase his impact on medicine. At that time, he had a growing fascination with finance and business. He talked with the head of the pharmaceutical division of Sandoz, who offered him the opportunity to join the company's US affiliate. In his five years in the United States, Vasella flourished in the stimulating environment, first as a sales representative and later as a product manager, and advanced rapidly through the Sandoz marketing organization.

When Sandoz merged with Ciba-Geigy in 1996, Vasella was named CEO of the combined companies, now called Novartis, despite his young age and limited experience. Once in the CEO's role, Vasella blossomed as a leader. He envisioned the opportunity to build a great global health care company that could help people through lifesaving new drugs, such as Gleevec, which has proved to be highly effective for patients with chronic myeloid leukemia. Drawing on the physician role models of his youth, he built an entirely new Novartis culture centered on compassion, competence, and competition. These moves established Novartis as a giant in the industry and Vasella as a compassionate leader.

Vasella's experience is just one of dozens provided by authentic leaders who traced their inspiration directly from their life stories. Asked what empowered them to lead, these leaders consistently replied that they found their strength through transformative experiences. Those experiences enabled them to understand the deeper purpose of their leadership.

Knowing your authentic self

When the 75 members of Stanford Graduate School of Business's Advisory Council were asked to recommend the most important capability for leaders to develop, their answer was nearly unanimous: self-awareness. Yet many leaders, especially those early in their careers, are trying so hard to establish themselves in the world that they leave little time for self-exploration. They strive to achieve success in tangible ways that are recognized in the external world—money, fame, power, status, or a rising stock price. Often their drive enables them to be professionally successful for a while, but they are unable to sustain that success. As they age, they may find something is missing in their lives and realize they are holding back from being the person they want to be. Knowing their authentic selves requires the courage and honesty to open up and examine their experiences. As they do so, leaders become more humane and willing to be vulnerable.

Of all the leaders we interviewed, David Pottruck, former CEO of Charles Schwab, had one of the most persistent journeys to self-awareness. An all-league football player in high school, Pottruck became MVP of his college team at the University of Pennsylvania. After completing his MBA at Wharton and a stint with Citigroup, he joined Charles Schwab as head of marketing, moving from New York to San Francisco. An extremely hard worker, Pottruck could not understand why his new colleagues resented the long hours he put in and his aggressiveness in pushing for results. "I thought my accomplishments would speak for themselves," he said. "It never occurred to me that my level of energy would intimidate and offend other people, because in my mind I was trying to help the company."

Pottruck was shocked when his boss told him, "Dave, your colleagues do not trust you." As he recalled, "That feedback was like a dagger to my heart. I was in denial, as I didn't see myself as others saw me. I became a lightning rod for friction, but I had no idea how self-serving I looked to other people. Still, somewhere in my inner core the feedback resonated as true." Pottruck realized that he could not succeed unless he identified and overcame his blind spots.

Denial can be the greatest hurdle that leaders face in becoming self-aware. They all have egos that need to be stroked, insecurities that need to be smoothed, fears that need to be allayed. Authentic leaders realize that they have to be willing to listen to feedback—especially the kind they don't want to hear. It was only after his second divorce that Pottruck finally was able to acknowledge that he still had large blind spots: "After my second marriage fell apart, I thought I had a wife-selection problem." Then he worked with a counselor who delivered some hard truths: "The good news is you do not have a wife-selection problem; the bad news is you have a husband-behavior problem." Pottruck then made a determined effort to change. As he described it, "I was like a guy who has had three heart attacks and finally realizes he has to quit smoking and lose some weight."

These days Pottruck is happily remarried and listens carefully when his wife offers constructive feedback. He acknowledges that he falls back on his old habits at times, particularly in high-stress situations, but now he has developed ways of coping with stress. "I have had enough success in life to have that foundation of self-respect, so I can take the criticism and not deny it. I have finally learned to tolerate my failures and disappointments and not beat myself up."

Practicing your values and principles

The values that form the basis for authentic leadership are derived from your beliefs and convictions, but you will not know what your true values are until they are tested under pressure. It is relatively easy to list your values and to live by them when things are going well. When your success, your career, or even your life hangs in the balance, you learn what is most important, what you are prepared to sacrifice, and what trade-offs you are willing to make.

Leadership principles are values translated into action. Having a solid base of values and testing them under fire enables you to develop the principles you will use in leading. For example, a value such as "concern for others" might be translated into a leadership principle such as "create a work environment where people are respected for their contributions, provided job security, and allowed to fulfill their potential."

Consider Jon Huntsman, the founder and chairman of Huntsman Corporation. His moral values were deeply challenged when he worked for the Nixon administration in 1972, shortly before Watergate. After a brief stint in the US Department of Health, Education, and Welfare (HEW), he took a job under H. R. Haldeman, President Nixon's powerful chief of staff. Huntsman said he found the experience of taking orders from Haldeman "very mixed. I wasn't geared to take orders, irrespective of whether they were ethically or morally right." He explained, "We had a few clashes, as plenty of things that Haldeman wanted to do were questionable. An amoral atmosphere permeated the White House."

One day, Haldeman directed Huntsman to help him entrap a California congressman who had been opposing a White House initiative. The congressman was part owner of a plant that reportedly employed undocumented workers. To gather information to embarrass the congressman, Haldeman told Huntsman to get the plant manager of a company Huntsman owned to place some undocumented workers at the congressman's plant in an undercover operation.

"There are times when we react too quickly and fail to realize immediately what is right and wrong," Huntsman recalled. "This was one of those times when I didn't think it through. I knew instinctively it was wrong, but it took a few minutes for the notion to percolate. After 15 minutes, my inner moral compass made itself noticed and enabled me to recognize this wasn't the right thing to do. Values that had accompanied me since childhood kicked in. Halfway through my conversation with our plant manager, I said to him, 'Let's not do this. I don't want to play this game. Forget that I called.'"

Huntsman told Haldeman that he would not use his employees in this way. "Here I was saying no to the second most powerful person in the country. He didn't appreciate responses like that, as he viewed

YOUR DEVELOPMENT AS AN AUTHENTIC LEADER

As you read this article, think about the basis for your leadership development and the path you need to follow to become an authentic leader. Then ask yourself these questions:

1. *Which people and experiences in your early life had the greatest impact on you?*

2. *What tools do you use to become self-aware?* What is your authentic self? What are the moments when you say to yourself, "This is the real me"?

3. *What are your most deeply held values?* Where did they come from? Have your values changed significantly since your childhood? How do your values inform your actions?

4. *What motivates you extrinsically?* What are your intrinsic motivations? How do you balance extrinsic and intrinsic motivation in your life?

(Continued)

21

YOUR DEVELOPMENT AS AN AUTHENTIC LEADER

5. *What kind of support team do you have?* How can your support team make you a more authentic leader? How should you diversify your team to broaden your perspective?

6. *Is your life integrated?* Are you able to be the same person in all aspects of your life— personal, work, family, and community? If not, what is holding you back?

7. *What does being authentic mean in your life?* Are you more effective as a leader when you behave authentically? Have you ever paid a price for your authenticity as a leader? Was it worth it?

8. *What steps can you take today, tomorrow, and over the next year to develop your authentic leadership?*

them as signs of disloyalty. I might as well have been saying farewell. So be it. I left within the next six months."

Balancing your extrinsic and intrinsic motivations

Because authentic leaders need to sustain high levels of motivation and keep their lives in balance, it is critically important for them to understand what drives them. There are two types of motivations—extrinsic and intrinsic. Although they are reluctant to admit it, many leaders are propelled to achieve by measuring their success against the outside world's parameters. They enjoy the recognition and status that come with promotions and financial rewards. Intrinsic motivations, on the other hand, are derived from their sense of the meaning of their life. They are closely linked to one's life story and the way one frames it. Examples include personal growth, helping other people develop, taking on social causes, and making a difference in the world. The key is to find a balance between your desires for external validation and the intrinsic motivations that provide fulfillment in your work.

Many interviewees advised aspiring leaders to be wary of getting caught up in social, peer, or parental expectations. Debra Dunn, who has worked in Silicon Valley for decades as a Hewlett-Packard executive, acknowledged the constant pressures from external sources: "The path of accumulating material possessions is clearly laid out. You know how to measure it. If you don't pursue that path, people wonder what is wrong with you. The only way to avoid getting caught up in materialism is to understand where you find happiness and fulfillment."

Moving away from the external validation of personal achievement is not always easy. Achievement-oriented leaders grow so accustomed to successive accomplishments throughout their early years that it takes courage to pursue their intrinsic motivations. But at some point, most leaders recognize that they need to address more difficult questions in order to pursue truly meaningful success. McKinsey's Alice Woodwark, who at 29 has already achieved notable success, reflected: "My version of achievement was pretty naive, born of things I learned early in life about praise and being valued. But if you're just chasing the rabbit around the course, you're not running toward anything meaningful."

Intrinsic motivations are congruent with your values and are more fulfilling than extrinsic motivations. John Thain, CEO of the New York Stock Exchange, said, "I am motivated by doing a really good job at whatever I am doing, but I prefer to multiply my impact on society through a group of people." Or as Ann Moore, chairman and CEO of Time, put it, "I came here 25 years ago solely because I loved magazines and the publishing world." Moore had a dozen job offers after business school but took the lowest-paying one with Time because of her passion for publishing.

Building your support team

Leaders cannot succeed on their own; even the most outwardly confident executives need support and advice. Without strong relationships to provide perspective, it is very easy to lose your way.

Authentic leaders build extraordinary support teams to help them stay on course. Those teams counsel them in times of uncertainty, help them in times of difficulty, and celebrate with them in times of success. After their hardest days, leaders find comfort in being with people on whom they can rely so they can be open and vulnerable. During the low points, they cherish the friends who appreciate them for who they are, not what they are. Authentic leaders find that their support teams provide affirmation, advice, perspective, and calls for course corrections when needed.

How do you go about building your support team? Most authentic leaders have a multifaceted support structure that includes their spouses or significant others, families, mentors, close friends, and colleagues. They build their networks over time, as the experiences, shared histories, and openness with people close to them create the trust and confidence they need in times of trial and uncertainty. Leaders must give as much to their supporters as they get from them so that mutually beneficial relationships can develop.

It starts with having at least one person in your life with whom you can be completely yourself, warts and all, and still be accepted unconditionally. Often that person is the only one who can tell you the honest truth. Most leaders have their closest relationships with their spouses, although some develop these bonds with another family member, a close friend, or a trusted mentor. When leaders can rely on unconditional support, they are more likely to accept themselves for who they really are.

Many relationships grow over time through an expression of shared values and a common purpose. Randy Komisar of venture capital firm Kleiner Perkins Caufield & Byers said his marriage to Hewlett-Packard's Debra Dunn is lasting because it is rooted in similar values. "Debra and I are very independent but extremely harmonious in terms of our personal aspirations, values, and principles. We have a strong resonance around questions like, 'What is your legacy in this world?' It is important to be in sync about what we do with our lives."

Many leaders have had a mentor who changed their lives. The best mentoring interactions spark mutual learning, exploration of similar values, and shared enjoyment. If people are only looking for a leg up from their mentors, instead of being interested in their mentors' lives as well, the relationships will not last for long. It is the two-way nature of the connection that sustains it.

Personal and professional support groups can take many forms. Piper Jaffray's Tad Piper is a member of an Alcoholics Anonymous group. He noted, "These are not CEOs. They are just a group of nice, hard-working people who are trying to stay sober, lead good lives, and work with each other about being open, honest, and vulnerable. We reinforce each other's behavior by talking about our chemical dependency in a disciplined way as we go through the 12 steps. I feel blessed to be surrounded by people who are thinking about those kinds of issues and actually doing something, not just talking about them."

Bill George's experiences echo Piper's: In 1974, he joined a men's group that formed after a weekend retreat. More than 30 years later, the group is still meeting every Wednesday morning. After an opening period of catching up on each other's lives and dealing with any particular difficulty someone may be facing, one of the group's eight members leads a discussion on a topic he has selected. These discussions are open, probing, and often profound. The key to their success is that people say what they really believe without fear of judgment, criticism, or reprisal. All the members consider the group to be one of the most important aspects of their lives, enabling them to clarify their beliefs, values, and understanding of vital issues, as well as serving as a source of honest feedback when they need it most.

Integrating your life by staying grounded

Integrating their lives is one of the greatest challenges leaders face. To lead a balanced life, you need to bring together all of its constituent elements—work, family, community, and friends—so that you can be the same person in each environment. Think of your life as a house, with a bedroom for your personal life, a study for your professional life, a family room for your family, and a living room to share with your friends. Can you knock down the walls between these rooms and be the same person in each of them?

As John Donahoe, president of eBay Marketplaces and former worldwide managing director of Bain, stressed, being authentic means maintaining a sense of self no matter where you are. He warned, "The world can shape you if you let it. To have a sense of yourself as you live, you must make conscious choices. Sometimes the choices are really hard, and you make a lot of mistakes."

Authentic leaders have a steady and confident presence. They do not show up as one person one day and another person the next. Integration takes discipline, particularly during stressful times when it is easy to become reactive and slip back into bad habits. Donahoe feels strongly that integrating his life has enabled him to become a more effective leader. "There is no nirvana," he said. "The struggle is constant, as the trade-offs don't get any easier as you get older." But for authentic leaders, personal and professional lives are not a zero-sum game. As Donahoe said, "I have no doubt today that my children have made me a far more effective leader in the workplace. Having a strong personal life has made the difference." Leading is high-stress work. There is no way to avoid stress when you are responsible for people, organizations, outcomes, and managing the constant uncertainties of the environment. The higher you go, the greater your freedom to control your destiny but also the higher the degree of stress. The question is not whether you can avoid stress but how you can control it to maintain your own sense of equilibrium.

Authentic leaders are constantly aware of the importance of staying grounded. Besides spending time with their families and close friends, authentic leaders get physical exercise, engage in spiritual practices, do community service, and return to the places where they grew up. All are essential to their effectiveness as leaders, enabling them to sustain their authenticity.

Empowering people to lead

Now that we have discussed the process of discovering your authentic leadership, let's look at how authentic leaders empower people in their organizations to achieve superior long-term results, which is the bottom line for all leaders.

Authentic leaders recognize that leadership is not about their success or about getting loyal subordinates to follow them. They know the key to a successful organization is having empowered leaders at all levels, including those who have no direct reports. They not only inspire those around them, they empower those individuals to step up and lead.

A reputation for building relationships and empowering people was instrumental in chairman and

CEO Anne Mulcahy's stunning turnaround of Xerox. When Mulcahy was asked to take the company's reins from her failed predecessor, Xerox had $18 billion in debt, and all credit lines were exhausted. With the share price in free fall, morale was at an all-time low. To make matters worse, the SEC was investigating the company's revenue recognition practices.

Mulcahy's appointment came as a surprise to everyone—including Mulcahy herself. A Xerox veteran, she had worked in field sales and on the corporate staff for 25 years, but not in finance, R&D, or manufacturing. How could Mulcahy cope with this crisis when she had had no financial experience? She brought to the CEO role the relationships she had built over 25 years, an impeccable understanding of the organization, and, above all, her credibility as an authentic leader. She bled for Xerox, and everyone knew it. Because of that, they were willing to go the extra mile for her.

After her appointment, Mulcahy met personally with the company's top 100 executives to ask them if they would stay with the company despite the challenges ahead. "I knew there were people who weren't supportive of me," she said. "So I confronted a couple of them and said, 'This is about the company.'"

The first two people Mulcahy talked with, both of whom ran big operating units, decided to leave, but the remaining 98 committed to stay. Throughout the crisis, people in Xerox were empowered by Mulcahy to step up and lead in order to restore the company to its former greatness. In the end, her leadership enabled Xerox to avoid bankruptcy as she paid back $10 billion in debt and restored revenue growth and profitability with a combination of cost savings and innovative new products. The stock price tripled as a result.

Like Mulcahy, all leaders have to deliver bottom-line results. By creating a virtuous circle in which the results reinforce the effectiveness of their leadership, authentic leaders are able to sustain those results through good times and bad. Their success enables them to attract talented people and align employees' activities with shared goals, as they empower others on their team to lead by taking on greater challenges. Indeed, superior results over a sustained period of time is the ultimate mark of an authentic leader. It may be possible to drive short-term outcomes without being authentic, but authentic leadership is the only way we know to create sustainable long-term results.

For authentic leaders, there are special rewards. No individual achievement can equal the pleasure of leading a group of people to achieve a worthy goal. When you cross the finish line together, all the pain and suffering you may have experienced quickly vanishes. It is replaced by a deep inner satisfaction that you have empowered others and thus made the world a better place. That's the challenge and the fulfillment of authentic leadership.

BILL GEORGE is a professor of management practice at Harvard Business School and the former chair and CEO of Medtronic. PETER SIMS is a management writer and entrepreneur. He is the author of *Little Bets: How Breakthrough Ideas Emerge from Small Discoveries*. He is also the founder of the BLK SHP. ANDREW N. MCLEAN is a research associate at Harvard Business School. DIANA MAYER is a former Citigroup executive in New York. This article was adapted from *True North: Discover Your Authentic Leadership* by Bill George with Peter Sims.

Reprinted from *Harvard Business Review*, February 2007 (product #R0702H).

2

The Authenticity Paradox

By Herminia Ibarra

Authenticity has become the gold standard for leadership. But a simplistic understanding of what it means can hinder your growth and limit your impact.

Consider Cynthia, a general manager in a health care organization. Her promotion into that role increased her direct reports tenfold and expanded the range of businesses she oversaw—and she felt a little shaky about making such a big leap. A strong believer in transparent, collaborative leadership, she bared her soul to her new employees: "I want to do this job," she said, "but it's scary, and I need your help." Her candor backfired; she lost credibility with people who wanted and needed a confident leader to take charge.

Or take George, a Malaysian executive in an auto parts company where people valued a clear chain of command and made decisions by consensus. When a Dutch multinational with a matrix structure acquired the company, George found himself working with peers who saw decision making as a freewheeling contest for the best-debated ideas. That style didn't come easily to him, and it contradicted everything he had learned about humility growing up in his country. In a 360-degree debrief, his boss told him that he needed to sell his ideas and accomplishments more aggressively. George felt he had to choose between being a failure and being a fake.

Because going against our natural inclinations can make us feel like impostors, we tend to latch on to authenticity as an excuse for sticking with what's comfortable. But few jobs allow us to do that for long. That's doubly true when we advance in our careers or when demands or expectations change, as Cynthia, George, and countless other executives have discovered.

In my research on leadership transitions, I have observed that career advances require all of us to move way beyond our comfort zones. At the same time, however, they trigger a strong countervailing impulse to protect our identities: When we are unsure of ourselves or our ability to perform well or measure up in a new setting, we often retreat to familiar behaviors and styles.

But my research also demonstrates that the moments that most challenge our sense of self are the ones that can teach us the most about leading effectively. By viewing ourselves as works in progress and evolving our professional identities through trial and error, we can develop a personal style that feels right to us and suits our organizations' changing needs.

That takes courage, because learning, by definition, starts with unnatural and often superficial behaviors that can make us feel calculating instead of genuine and spontaneous. But the only way to avoid being pigeonholed and ultimately become better leaders is to do the things that a rigidly authentic sense of self would keep us from doing.

Why leaders struggle with authenticity

The word "authentic" traditionally referred to any work of art that is an original, not a copy. When used to describe leadership, of course, it has other meanings—and they can be problematic. For example, the notion of adhering to one "true self" flies in the face of much research on how people evolve with experience, discovering facets of themselves they would never have unearthed through introspection alone. And being utterly transparent—disclosing every single thought and feeling—is both unrealistic and risky. (See figure 1, "What is authenticity?")

FIGURE 1

What is authenticity?

A too-rigid definition of authenticity can get in the way of effective leadership. Here are three examples and the problems they pose.

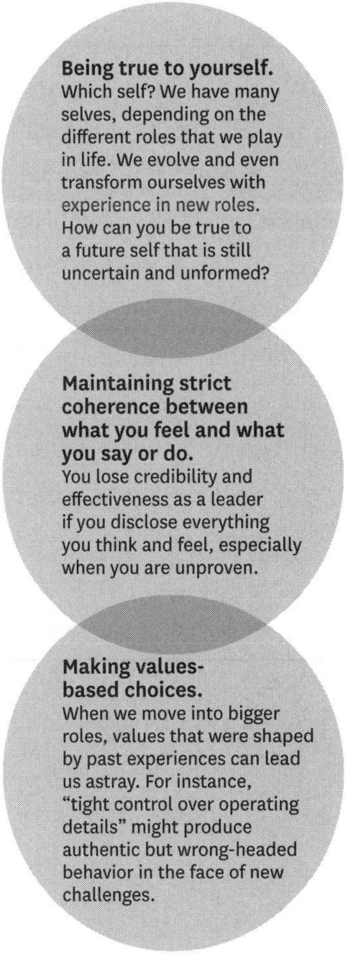

Being true to yourself.
Which self? We have many selves, depending on the different roles that we play in life. We evolve and even transform ourselves with experience in new roles. How can you be true to a future self that is still uncertain and unformed?

Maintaining strict coherence between what you feel and what you say or do.
You lose credibility and effectiveness as a leader if you disclose everything you think and feel, especially when you are unproven.

Making values-based choices.
When we move into bigger roles, values that were shaped by past experiences can lead us astray. For instance, "tight control over operating details" might produce authentic but wrong-headed behavior in the face of new challenges.

Leaders today struggle with authenticity for several reasons. First, we make more-frequent and more-radical changes in the kinds of work we do. As we strive to *improve* our game, a clear and firm sense of self is a compass that helps us navigate choices and progress toward our goals. But when we're looking to *change* our game, a too-rigid self-concept becomes an anchor that keeps us from sailing forth, as it did at first with Cynthia.

Second, in global business, many of us work with people who don't share our cultural norms and have different expectations for how we should behave. It can often seem as if we have to choose between what is expected—and therefore effective—and what feels authentic. George is a case in point.

Third, identities are always on display in today's world of ubiquitous connectivity and social media. How we present ourselves—not just as executives but as people, with quirks and broader interests—has become an important aspect of leadership. Having to carefully curate a persona that's out there for all to see can clash with our private sense of self.

In dozens of interviews with talented executives facing new expectations, I have found that they most often grapple with authenticity in the following situations.

Taking charge in an unfamiliar role

As everyone knows, the first 90 days are critical in a new leadership role. First impressions form quickly, and they matter. Depending on their personalities, leaders respond very differently to the increased visibility and performance pressure.

Psychologist Mark Snyder, of the University of Minnesota, identified two psychological profiles that inform how leaders develop their personal styles. "High self-monitors"—or chameleons, as I call them— are naturally able and willing to adapt to the demands of a situation without feeling fake. Chameleons care about managing their public image and often mask their vulnerability with bluster. They may not always get it right the first time, but they keep trying on different styles like new clothes until they find a good fit for themselves and their circumstances. Because of that flexibility, they often advance rapidly. But chameleons can run into problems when people perceive them as disingenuous or lacking a moral center—even though they're expressing their "true" chameleon nature.

By contrast, "true-to-selfers" (Snyder's "low self-monitors") tend to express what they really think and feel, even when it runs counter to situational demands. The danger with true-to-selfers like Cynthia and George is that they may stick too long with comfortable behavior that prevents them from meeting new requirements, instead of evolving their style as they gain insight and experience.

Cynthia (whom I interviewed after her story appeared in a *Wall Street Journal* article by Carol Hymowitz) hemmed herself in like this. She thought she was setting herself up for success by staying true to her highly personal, full-disclosure style of management. She asked her new team for support, openly acknowledging that she felt a bit at sea. As she scrambled to learn unfamiliar aspects of the business, she worked tirelessly to contribute to every decision and solve every problem. After a few months, she was on the verge of burnout. To make matters worse, sharing her vulnerability with her team members so early on had damaged her standing. Reflecting on her transition some years later, Cynthia told me: "Being authentic doesn't mean that you can be held up to the light and people can see right through you." But at the time, that was how she saw it—and instead of building trust, she made people question her ability to do the job.

Delegating and communicating appropriately are only part of the problem in a case like this. A deeper-seated issue is finding the right mix of distance and closeness in an unfamiliar situation. Stanford psychologist Deborah Gruenfeld describes this as managing the tension between authority and approachability. To be authoritative, you privilege your knowledge, experience, and expertise over the team's, maintaining a measure of distance. To be approachable, you emphasize your relationships with people, their input, and their perspective, and you lead with empathy and warmth. Getting the balance right presents an acute authenticity crisis for true-to-selfers, who typically have a strong preference for behaving one way or the other. Cynthia made herself too approachable and vulnerable, and it undermined and drained her. In her bigger role, she needed more distance from her employees to gain their confidence and get the job done.

Selling your ideas (and yourself)

Leadership growth usually involves a shift from having good ideas to pitching them to diverse stakeholders. Inexperienced leaders, especially true-to-selfers, often find the process of getting buy-in distasteful because it feels artificial and political; they believe that their work should stand on its own merits.

Here's an example: Anne, a senior manager at a transportation company, had doubled revenue and fundamentally redesigned core processes in her unit. Despite her obvious accomplishments, however, her boss didn't consider her an inspirational leader. Anne also knew she was not communicating effectively in her role as a board member of the parent company. The chairman, a broad-brush thinker, often became impatient with her detail orientation. His feedback to her was "step up, do the vision thing." But to Anne that seemed like valuing form over substance. "For me, it is manipulation," she told me in an interview. "I can do the storytelling too, but I refuse to play on people's emotions. If the string-pulling is too obvious, I can't make myself do it." Like many aspiring leaders, she resisted crafting emotional messages to influence and inspire others because that felt less authentic to her than relying on facts, figures, and spreadsheets. As a result, she worked at cross-purposes with the board chairman, pushing hard on the facts instead of pulling him in as a valued ally.

Many managers know deep down that their good ideas and strong potential will go unnoticed if they don't do a better job of selling themselves. Still, they can't bring themselves to do it. "I try to build a network based on professionalism and what I can deliver for the business, not who I know," one manager told me. "Maybe that's not smart from a career point of view. But I can't go against my beliefs . . . So I have been more limited in 'networking up.'"

Until we see career advancement as a way of extending our reach and increasing our impact in the organization—a collective win, not just a selfish pursuit—we have trouble feeling authentic when touting our strengths to influential people. True-to-selfers find it particularly hard to sell themselves to senior management when they most need to do so: when they are still unproven. Research shows, however, that this hesitancy disappears as people gain experience and become more certain of the value they bring.

Processing negative feedback

Many successful executives encounter serious negative feedback for the first time in their careers when they take on larger roles or responsibilities. Even when the criticisms aren't exactly new, they loom larger because the stakes are higher. But leaders often convince themselves that dysfunctional aspects of their "natural" style are the inevitable price of being effective.

Let's look at Jacob, a food company production manager whose direct reports gave him low marks in a 360 review on emotional intelligence, team building, and empowering others. One team member wrote that it was hard for Jacob to accept criticism.

Another remarked that after an angry outburst, he'd suddenly make a joke as if nothing had happened, not realizing the destabilizing effect of his mood changes on those around him. For someone who genuinely believed that he'd built trust among his people, all this was tough to swallow.

Once the initial shock had subsided, Jacob acknowledged that this was not the first time he'd received such criticism (some colleagues and subordinates had made similar comments a few years earlier). "I thought I'd changed my approach," he reflected, "but I haven't really changed so much since the last time." However, he quickly rationalized his behavior to his boss: "Sometimes you have to be tough in order to deliver results, and people don't like it," he said. "You have to accept that as part of the job description." Of course, he was missing the point. Because negative feedback given to leaders often centers on style rather than skills or expertise, it can feel like a threat to their identity—as if they're being

WHY COMPANIES ARE PUSHING AUTHENTICITY TRAINING

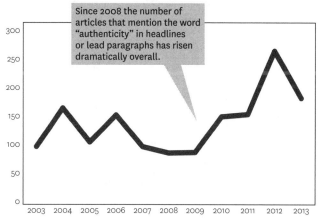

Since 2008 the number of articles that mention the word "authenticity" in headlines or lead paragraphs has risen dramatically overall.

Source: New York Times, Financial Times, Washington Post, Economic Post, Forbes, Wall Street Journal, and HBR

Managers can choose from countless books, articles, and executive workshops for advice on how to be more authentic at work. Two trends help explain the exploding popularity of the concept and the training industry it has fed.

(Continued)

WHY COMPANIES ARE PUSHING AUTHENTICITY TRAINING

First, trust in business leaders fell to an all-time low in 2012, according to the Edelman Trust Barometer. Even in 2013, when trust began to climb back up, only 18% of people reported that they trusted business leaders to tell the truth, and fewer than half trusted businesses to do the right thing.

Second, employee engagement is at a nadir. A 2013 Gallup poll found that only 13% of employees worldwide are engaged at work. Only one in eight workers—out of roughly 180 million employees studied—is psychologically committed to his or her job. In study after study, frustration, burnout, disillusionment, and misalignment with personal values are cited among the biggest reasons for career change.

At a time when public confidence and employee morale are so low, it's no surprise that companies are encouraging leaders to discover their "true" selves.

asked to give up their "secret sauce." That's how Jacob saw it. Yes, he could be explosive—but from his point of view, his "toughness" allowed him to deliver results year after year. In reality, though, he had succeeded up to this point *despite* his behavior. When his role expanded and he took on greater responsibility, his intense scrutiny of subordinates became an even bigger obstacle because it took up time he should have been devoting to more-strategic pursuits.

A great public example of this phenomenon is Margaret Thatcher. Those who worked with her knew she could be merciless if someone failed to prepare as thoroughly as she did. She was capable of humiliating a staff member in public, she was a notoriously bad listener, and she believed that compromise was cowardice. As she became known to the world as the "Iron Lady," Thatcher grew more and more convinced of the rightness of her ideas and the necessity of her coercive methods. She could beat anyone into submission with the power of her rhetoric and conviction, and she only got better at it. Eventually, though, it was her undoing—she was ousted by her own cabinet.

A playful frame of mind

Such a rigid self-concept can result from too much introspection. When we look only within for answers, we inadvertently reinforce old ways of seeing the world and outdated views of ourselves. Without the benefit of what I call outsight—the valuable external perspective we get from experimenting with new leadership behaviors—habitual patterns of thought and action fence us in. To begin thinking like leaders, we must first act: plunge ourselves into new projects and activities, interact with very different kinds of people, and experiment with new ways of getting things done. Especially in times of transition and uncertainty, thinking and introspection should follow experience—not vice versa. Action changes who we are and what we believe is worth doing.

Fortunately, there are ways of increasing outsight and evolving toward an "adaptively authentic" way of leading, but they require a playful frame of mind. Think of leadership development as trying on possible selves rather than working on yourself—which, let's face it, sounds like drudgery. When we adopt a playful attitude, we're more open to possibilities. It's OK to be inconsistent from one day to the next. That's not being a fake; it's how we experiment to figure out what's right for the new challenges and circumstances we face.

My research suggests three important ways to get started.

Learn from diverse role models

Most learning necessarily involves some form of imitation—and the understanding that nothing is "original." An important part of growing as a leader is viewing authenticity not as an intrinsic state but as the ability to take elements you have learned from others' styles and behaviors and make them your own.

But don't copy just one person's leadership style; tap many diverse role models. There is a big difference between imitating someone wholesale and borrowing selectively from various people to create your own collage, which you then modify and improve. As the playwright Wilson Mizner said, copying one author is plagiarism, but copying many is research.

I observed the importance of this approach in a study of investment bankers and consultants who were advancing from analytical and project work to roles advising clients and selling new business. Though most of them felt incompetent and insecure in their new positions, the chameleons among them consciously borrowed styles and tactics from successful senior leaders—learning through emulation how to use humor to break tension in meetings, for instance, and how to shape opinion without being overbearing. Essentially, the chameleons faked it until they found what worked for them. Noticing their efforts, their managers provided coaching and mentoring and shared tacit knowledge.

As a result, the chameleons arrived much faster at an authentic but more skillful style than the true-to-selfers in the study, who continued to focus solely on demonstrating technical mastery. Often the true-to-selfers concluded that their managers were "all talk and little content" and therefore not suitable role models. In the absence of a "perfect" model they had a harder time with imitation—it felt bogus. Unfortunately, their managers perceived their inability to adapt as a lack of effort or investment and thus didn't give them as much mentoring and coaching as they gave the chameleons.

Work on getting better

Setting goals for learning (not just for performance) helps us experiment with our identities without feeling like impostors, because we don't expect to get everything right from the start. We stop trying to protect our comfortable old selves from the threats that change can bring and start exploring what kinds of leaders we might become.

Of course, we all want to perform well in a new situation—get the right strategy in place, execute like crazy, deliver results the organization cares about. But focusing exclusively on those things makes us afraid to take risks in the service of learning. In a series of ingenious experiments, Stanford psychologist Carol Dweck has shown that concern about how we will appear to others inhibits learning on new or unfamiliar tasks. Performance goals motivate us to show others that we possess valued attributes, such as intelligence and social skill, and to prove to ourselves that we

THE CULTURAL FACTOR

Whatever the situation—taking charge in unfamiliar territory, selling your ideas and yourself, or processing negative feedback—finding authentic ways of being effective is even more difficult in a multicultural environment.

As my INSEAD colleague Erin Meyer finds in her research, styles of persuading others and the kinds of arguments that people find persuasive are far from universal; they are deeply rooted in a culture's philosophical, religious, and educational assumptions. That said, prescriptions for how leaders are supposed to look and sound are rarely as diverse as the leaders themselves. And despite corporate initiatives to build understanding of cultural differences and promote diversity, the fact is that leaders are still expected to express ideas assertively, to claim credit for them, and to use charisma to motivate and inspire people.

(Continued)

THE CULTURAL FACTOR

Authenticity is supposed to be an antidote to a single model of leadership. (After all, the message is to be yourself, not what someone else expects you to be.) But as the notion has gained currency, it has, ironically, come to mean something much more limiting and culturally specific. A closer look at how leaders are taught to discover and demonstrate authenticity—by telling a personal story about a hardship they have overcome, for example—reveals a model that is, in fact, very American, based on ideals such as self-disclosure, humility, and individualistic triumph over adversity.

This amounts to a catch-22 for managers from cultures with different norms for authority, communication, and collective endeavor because they must behave inauthentically in order to conform to the strictures of "authentic" leadership.

have them. By contrast, learning goals motivate us to develop valued attributes.

When we're in performance mode, leadership is about presenting ourselves in the most favorable light. In learning mode, we can reconcile our yearning for authenticity in how we work and lead with an equally powerful desire to grow. One leader I met was highly effective in small-group settings but struggled to convey openness to new ideas in larger meetings, where he often stuck to long-winded presentations for fear of getting derailed by others' comments. He set himself a "no PowerPoint" rule to develop a more relaxed, improvisational style. He surprised himself by how much he learned, not only about his own evolving preferences but also about the issues at hand.

Don't stick to "your story"

Most of us have personal narratives about defining moments that taught us important lessons. Consciously or not, we allow our stories, and the images of ourselves that they paint, to guide us in new situations. But the stories can become outdated as we grow, so sometimes it's necessary to alter them dramatically or even to throw them out and start from scratch.

That was true for Maria, a leader who saw herself as a "mother hen with her chicks all around." Her coach, former Ogilvy & Mather CEO Charlotte Beers, explains in *I'd Rather Be in Charge* that this self-image emerged from a time when Maria had to sacrifice her own goals and dreams to take care of her extended family. It eventually began to hold her back in her career: Though it had worked for her as a friendly and loyal team player and a peacekeeper, it wasn't helping her get the big leadership assignment she wanted. Together Maria and her coach looked for another defining moment to use as a touchstone— one that was more in keeping with Maria's desired future self, not who she had been in the past. They chose the time when Maria, as a young woman, had left her family to travel the world for 18 months. Acting from that bolder sense of self, she asked for—and got—a promotion that had previously been elusive.

Dan McAdams, a Northwestern psychology professor who has spent his career studying life stories, describes identity as "the internalized and evolving story that results from a person's selective appropriation of past, present, and future." This isn't just academic jargon. McAdams is saying that you have to believe your story—but also embrace how it changes over time, according to what you need it to do. Try out new stories about yourself, and keep editing them, much as you would your résumé.

Again, revising one's story is both an introspective and a social process. The narratives we choose should not only sum up our experiences and aspirations but also reflect the demands we face and resonate with the audience we're trying to win over.

Countless books and advisers tell you to start your leadership journey with a clear sense of who you are. But that can be a recipe for staying stuck in the past. Your leadership identity can and should change each time you move on to bigger and better things.

The only way we grow as leaders is by stretching the limits of who we are—doing new things that make us uncomfortable but that teach us through direct experience who we want to become. Such growth doesn't require a radical personality make-over. Small changes—in the way we carry ourselves, the way we communicate, the way we interact—often make a world of difference in how effectively we lead.

HERMINIA IBARRA is a professor of organizational behavior and the Cora Chaired Professor of Leadership and Learning at INSEAD. She is the author of *Act Like a Leader, Think Like a Leader* (Harvard Business Review Press, 2015) and *Working Identity: Unconventional Strategies for Reinventing*

Your Career (Harvard Business School Press, 2003). Follow her on Twitter @HerminiaIbarra and visit her website www .herminiaibarra.com.

Reprinted from *Harvard Business Review*,
January–February 2015 (product #R1501C).

3

What Bosses Gain by Being Vulnerable

By Emma Seppala

One morning in Bangalore, South India, Archana Patchirajan, founder of a technology startup, called her entire staff in for a meeting. When everyone was seated, she announced that she had to let them go because the startup had run out of funds. She could no longer pay them. Shockingly, her staff of high-caliber engineers who had their pick of jobs in the booming Silicon Valley of India, refused to go. They said they would rather work for half their pay than leave her. They stayed and kept working so hard that, a few years later, Patchirajan's company—Hubbl, which provides internet advertising solutions—sold for $14 million.

Patchirajan continues to work on startups from the United States, and her staff, though thousands of miles away from her, continues to work for her.

What explains the connection and devotion that Patchirajan's staff had toward her?

Patchirajan's story is particularly extraordinary when you consider the alarming fact that according to a Gallup study, 70% of employees are "not engaged" or are "actively disengaged" at work.[1] As a consequence, they are "less emotionally connected" and also "less likely to be productive." What is it about Patchirajan that not only prevented this phenomenon in her staff but actually flipped it?

When I asked one of Patchirajan's longest-standing employees what drove him and the rest of the team to stay with her, these are some of the things he shared: "We all work as a family because she treats us as such." "She knows everyone in the office and has a personal relationship with each one of us." "She does not get upset when we make mistakes but gives us the time to learn how to analyze and fix the situation."

If you look at these comments, they suggest that Patchirajan's relationship with her employees runs deeper than that of the usual employer-employee relationship. Simply put, she is vulnerable and authentic with them. She shared her doubts honestly when the company was going downhill, she does not adhere to a strict hierarchy but treats her employees like family members, and she has a personal relationship with each one of them. Sound touchy-feely, daunting, or counterintuitive? Here's why it's not.

Brené Brown, an expert on social connection, conducted thousands of interviews to discover what lies at the root of social connections. A thorough analysis of the data revealed what it was: vulnerability. Vulnerability here does not mean being weak or submissive. To the contrary, it implies the courage to be oneself. It means replacing "professional distance and cool" with uncertainty, risk, and emotional exposure. Opportunities for vulnerability present themselves to us at work every day. Some examples Patchirajan gives of vulnerability include calling an employee or colleague whose child is not well, reaching out to someone who has just had a loss in their family, asking someone for help, taking responsibility for something that went wrong at work, or sitting by the bedside of a colleague or employee with a terminal illness.

More important, Brown describes vulnerability and authenticity as being at the root of human connection. And human connection is often dramatically absent from workplaces. Johann Berlin, CEO of Transformational Leadership for Excellence (TLEX), recounts an experience he had while teaching a workshop at a *Fortune* 100 company. The participants were all higher-level management. After an exercise in which pairs of participants shared an event from their life with each other, one of the top executive managers approached Berlin. Visibly moved by the experience, he said "I've worked with my colleague for more than 25 years and have never known about the difficult times in his life." In a short moment of authentic connection, this manager's understanding and connection with his colleague deepened in ways that hadn't happened in decades of working together.

Why is human connection missing at work? As leaders and employees, we are often taught to keep a distance and project a certain image—one of confidence, competence, and authority. We may disclose our vulnerability to a spouse or close friend behind closed doors at night, but we would never show it elsewhere during the day, let alone at work.

However, data suggests that we may want to revisit the idea of projecting an image. Research shows that people subconsciously register a lack of authenticity in others. Just by looking at someone, we download large amounts of information. "We are programmed to observe each other's states so we can more appropriately interact, empathize, or assert our boundaries—whatever the situation may require," says Paula Niedenthal, professor of psychology at the University of Wisconsin–Madison. We are wired to read each others' expressions in a very nuanced way. This process is called "resonance," and it is so automatic and rapid that it often happens below our awareness.

Like an acute sounding board, parts of our brain internally echo what others do and feel. Just by looking at someone, you experience them: You internally resonate with them. Ever seen someone trip and momentarily felt a twinge of pain for them? Observing them activates the "pain matrix" in your brain, research shows.[2] Ever been moved by the sight of a person helping someone? You vicariously experienced it and thereby felt elevation. Someone's smile activates the smile muscles in our face, while a frown activates our frown muscles, according to research by Ulf Dimberg at Uppsala University in Sweden.[3] We internally register what another person is feeling. As a consequence, if a smile is fake, we are more likely to feel uncomfortable than comfortable.

While we may try to appear perfect, strong, or intelligent to be respected by others, pretense often has the opposite effect intended. Paula Niedenthal's research shows that we resonate too deeply with one another to ignore inauthenticity.[4] Just think of how uncomfortable you feel around someone you perceive as "taking on airs" or "putting on a show." We tend to see right through them and feel less connected. Or think of how you respond when you know someone is upset, but they're trying to conceal it. "What's wrong?" you ask, only to be told, "Nothing!" Rarely does this answer satisfy—because we sense it's not true.

Our brains are wired to read cues so subtle that even when we don't consciously register the cues, our bodies respond. For example, when someone is angry but keeps their feelings bottled up, we may not realize that they are angry (they don't *look* angry) but still our blood pressure will increase, according to research by James Gross at Stanford University.[5]

Why do we feel more comfortable around someone who is authentic and vulnerable? Because we are particularly sensitive to signs of trustworthiness in our leaders.[6] Servant leadership, for example, which is characterized by authenticity and values-based leadership, yields more positive and constructive behavior in employees and greater feelings of hope and trust in both the leader and the organization.[7] In turn, trust in a leader improves employee performance.[8] You can even see this at the level of the brain. Employees who recall a boss who resonated with them show enhanced activation in parts of the brain related to positive emotion and social connection.[9] The reverse is true when they think of a boss who did not resonate.

One example of authenticity and vulnerability is forgiveness. Forgiveness doesn't mean tolerance of error but rather a patient encouragement of growth.

Forgiveness is what Archana Patchirajan's employee described as, "She does not get upset when we make mistakes but gives us the time to learn how to analyze and fix the situation." Forgiveness may be another soft-sounding term but, as University of Michigan researcher Kim Cameron points out in the book *Positive Organizational Behavior*, it has hard results: A culture of forgiveness in organizations can lead to increased employee productivity as well as less voluntary turnover.[10] Again, a culture that is forgiving breeds trust. As a consequence, an organization becomes more resilient in times of organizational stress or downsizing.

Why do we fear vulnerability or think it's inappropriate for the workplace? For one, we are afraid that if someone finds out who we really are or discovers a soft or vulnerable spot, they will take advantage of us. However, as I describe in my hbr.org article, "The Hard Data on Being a Nice Boss," kindness goes further than the old sink-or-swim paradigm.

Here's what may happen if you embrace an authentic and vulnerable stance: Your staff will see you as a human being; they may feel closer to you, they may be prompted to share advice, and—if you are attached to hierarchy—you may find that your team begins to feel more horizontal. While these types of changes might feel uncomfortable, you may see, as in Patchirajan's case, that the benefits are worth it.

There are additional benefits you may reap from a closer connection to employees, too. One study out of Stanford shows that CEOs are looking for more advice and counsel but that two thirds of them don't get it.[11] This isolation can skew perspectives and lead to potentially disadvantageous leadership choices. Who better to receive advice from than your own employees, who are intimately familiar with your product, your customers, and problems that might exist within the organization?

Rather than feeling like another peg in the system, your team members will feel respected and honored for their opinions and will consequently become more loyal. The research shows that the personal connection and happiness employees derive from their work fosters greater loyalty than the amount on their paycheck.[12]

EMMA SEPPALA, PH.D., is the science director of Stanford University's Center for Compassion and Altruism Research and Education and author of *The Happiness Track*. She is also founder of Fulfillment Daily. Follow her on Twitter @emmaseppala or her website www.emmaseppala.com.

Notes

1. "Report: State of the American Workplace," Gallup poll, September 22, 2014, http://www.gallup.com/services/176708/state-american-workplace.aspx.
2. C. Lamm et al., "What Are You Feeling? Using Functional Magnetic Resonance Imaging to Assess the Modulation of Sensory and Affective Responses During Empathy for Pain," *PLOS One* 2, no. 12 (2007): e1292.
3. U. Dimberg, M. Thunberg, K. Elmehed, "Unconscious Facial Reactions to Emotional Facial Expressions," *Psychological Science* 11, no. 1 (2000): 86–89.

4. S. Korb et al., "The Perception and Mimicry of Facial Movements Predict Judgments of Smile Authenticity," *PLOS One* 9, no. 6 (2014): e99194.

5. J. Gross and R. Levenson, "Emotional Suppression: Physiology, Self-Report, and Expressive Behavior," *Journal of Personality and Social Psychology* 64, no. 6 (1993): 970–986.

6. K. Dirks and D. Ferrin, "Trust in Leadership: Meta-Analytic Findings and Implications for Research and Practice," *Journal of Applied Psychology* 87, no. 4 (2002): 611–628.

7. E. Joseph and B. Winston, "A Correlation of Servant Leadership, Leader Trust, and Organizational Trust," *Leadership & Organization Development Journal* 26, no. 1 (2005): 6–22; T. Searle and J. Barbuto, "Servant Leadership, Hope, and Organizational Virtuousness: A Framework Exploring Positive Micro and Macro Behaviors and Performance Impact," *Journal of Leadership & Organizational Studies* 18, no. 1 (2011): 107–117.

8. T. Bartram and G. Casimir, "The Relationship Between Leadership and Follower In-Role Performance and Satisfaction with the Leader: The Mediating Effects of Empowerment and Trust in the Leader," *Leadership & Organization Development Journal* 28, no. 1 (2007): 4–19.

9. R. Boyatzis et al., "Examination of the Neural Substrates Activated in Memories of Experiences with Resonant and Dissonant Leaders," *The Leadership Quarterly* 23, no. 2 (2012): 259–272.

10. K. Cameron, "Forgiveness in Organizations," *Positive Organizational Behavior*, ed. D. L. Nelson and C. L. Cooper (London: Sage Publications, 2007), 129–142.

11. Stanford GSB staff, "David Larcker: 'Lonely at the Top' Resonates for Most CEOs," *Insights* by Stanford Graduate School of Business, July 31, 2013, https://www.gsb.stanford.edu/insights/david-larcker-lonely-top-resonates-most-ceos.

12. The Association of Accounting Technicians, "Britain's Workers Value Companionship and Recognition Over a Big Salary, a Recent Report Revealed," July 15, 2014, https://www.aat.org.uk/about-aat/press-releases/britains-workers-value-companionship-recognition-over-big-salary.

Adapted from content posted on hbr.org,
December 11, 2014 (product #H01R7U).

4

Practice Tough Empathy

By Rob Goffee and Gareth Jones

There's altogether too much hype nowadays about the idea that leaders *must* show concern for their teams. There's nothing worse than seeing a manager return from the latest interpersonal-skills training program with "concern" for others. Real leaders don't need a training program to convince their employees that they care. Real leaders empathize fiercely with the people they lead. They also care intensely about the work their employees do.

Consider Alain Levy, the former CEO of Polygram. Although he often comes across as a rather aloof intellectual, Levy is well able to close the distance between himself and his followers. On one occasion, he helped some junior record executives in Australia choose singles off albums. Picking singles is a critical task in the music business: The selection of a song can make or break the album. Levy sat down with the young people and took on the work with passion. "You bloody idiots," he added his voice to the melee, "you don't know what the hell you're talking about; we always have a dance track first!" Within 24 hours, the story spread throughout the company; it was the best PR Levy ever got. "Levy really knows how to pick singles," people said. In fact, he knew how to identify with the work, and he knew how to enter his followers' world—one where strong, colorful language is the norm—to show them that he cared.

Clearly, as the above example illustrates, we do not believe that the empathy of inspirational leaders is the soft kind described in so much of the management literature. On the contrary, we feel that real leaders manage through a unique approach we call tough empathy. Tough empathy means giving people what they need, not what they want. Organizations like the Marine Corps and consulting firms specialize in tough empathy. Recruits are pushed to be the best that they can be; "grow or go" is the motto. Chris Satterwaite, the CEO of Bell Pottinger Communications and a former chief executive of several ad agencies, understands what tough empathy is all about. He adeptly handles the challenges of managing creative people while making tough decisions. "If I have to, I can be ruthless," he says. "But while they're with me, I promise my people that they'll learn."

At its best, tough empathy balances respect for the individual and for the task at hand. Attending to both, however, isn't easy, especially when the business is in survival mode. At such times, caring leaders have to give selflessly to the people around them and know when to pull back. Consider a situation at Unilever at a time when it was developing Persil Power, a detergent that eventually had to be removed from the market because it destroyed clothes that were laundered in it. Even though the product was show-ing early signs of trouble, CEO Niall FitzGerald stood by his troops. "That was the popular place to be, but I should not have been there," he says now. "I should have stood back, cool and detached, looked at the whole field, watched out for the customer." But caring with detachment is not easy, especially since, when done right, tough empathy is harder on you than on your employees. "Some theories of leadership make caring look effortless. It isn't," says Paulanne Man-cuso, president and CEO of Calvin Klein Cosmet-ics. "You have to do things you don't want to do, and that's hard." It's tough to be tough.

Tough empathy also has the benefit of impelling leaders to take risks. When Greg Dyke took over at the BBC, his commercial competitors were able to spend substantially more on programs than the BBC could. Dyke quickly realized that in order to thrive in a digital world, the BBC needed to increase its expenditures. He explained this openly and directly to the staff. Once he had secured their buy-in, he began thoroughly restructuring the organization. Although many employees were let go, he was able to maintain people's commitment. Dyke attributed his success to his tough empathy with employees: "Once you have the people with you, you can make the difficult decisions that need to be made."

One final point about tough empathy: Those more apt to use it are people who really care about something. And when people care deeply about something—anything—they're more likely to show their true selves. They will not only communicate authenticity, which is the precondition for leadership, but they will show that they are doing more than just playing a role. People do not commit to executives who merely live up to the obligations of their jobs. They want more. They want someone who cares passionately about the people and the work—just as they do.

ROB GOFFEE is Emeritus Professor of Organisational Behaviour at London Business School, where he teaches in the world-renowned Senior Executive Programme. GARETH JONES is a Fellow of the Centre for Management Development at London Business School and a visiting professor at Spain's IE Business School in Madrid. Goffee and Jones consult to the boards of several global companies and are coauthors of *Why Should Anyone Be Led by You?*, *Clever*, and *Why Should Anyone Work Here?*, all published by Harvard Business Review Press.

Excerpted from "Why Should Anyone Be
Led By You?" in *Harvard Business Review*,
September–October 2000 (product #R00506).

5

Cracking the Code That Stalls People of Color

By Sylvia Ann Hewlett

t's a topic that corporations once routinely ignored, then dismissed, and are only now beginning to discuss: the dearth of professionals of color in senior positions. Professionals of color hold only 11% of executive posts in corporate America.[1] Among *Fortune* 500 CEOs, only six are black, eight are Asian, and eight are Hispanic.[2]

Performance and hard work, along with sponsors, get top talent recognized and promoted, but leadership potential isn't enough to lever men and women into the executive suite. Top jobs are given to those who also look and act the part, who manifest "executive presence" (EP). According to research by the Center for Talent Innovation (CTI), EP constitutes 26% of what senior leaders say it takes to get the next promotion.[3] Yet because senior leaders are overwhelmingly Caucasian, professionals of color (African American, Asian, and Hispanic individuals) find themselves at an immediate disadvantage in trying to look, sound, and act like a leader. And the feedback that might help them do so is markedly absent at all levels of management.

Executive presence rests on three pillars: gravitas (the core characteristic, according to 67% of the 268 senior executives surveyed), an amalgam of behaviors that convey confidence, inspire trust, and bolster credibility; communication skills (according to 28%); and appearance, the filter through which communication skills and gravitas become more apparent. While they are aware of the importance of EP, men and women of color are nonetheless hard-pressed to interpret and embody aspects of a code written by and for white men.

Research from CTI finds that professionals of color, like their Caucasian counterparts, prioritize gravitas over communication and communication over appearance. Yet, "cracking the code" of executive presence presents unique challenges for professionals of color because standards of appropriate behavior, speech, and attire demand they suppress or sacrifice aspects of their cultural identity in order to conform. They overwhelmingly feel that EP at their firm is based on white male standards—African Americans, especially, were 97% more likely than their Caucasian counterparts to agree with this assessment—and that conforming to these standards requires altering their authenticity, a new version of "bleached-out professionalism" that contributes to feelings of resentment and disengagement. (See figures 2 and 3.) People of color already feel they have to work harder than their

FIGURE 2

Executive presence at my company is defined as conforming to traditionally white male standards

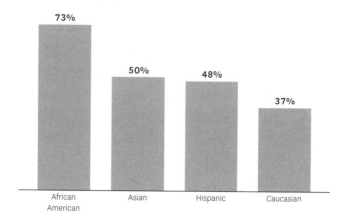

Source: Center for Talent Innovation

Caucasian counterparts just to be perceived as being on a par with them; more than half (56%) of minority professionals also feel they are held to a stricter code of EP standards.

FIGURE 3

I feel the need to compromise my authenticity to conform to executive presence standards at my company

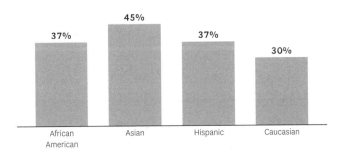

Source: Center for Talent Innovation

Executive presence further eludes professionals of color because they're not likely to get feedback on their "presentation of self." Qualitative findings affirm that their superiors, most of whom are white, hesitate to call attention to gravitas shortfalls or communication blunders for fear of coming across as racially insensitive or discriminatory. While sponsors might close this gap by specifically addressing EP issues with their high potentials, CTI's 2012 research shows that professionals of color are much less likely to have a sponsor than Caucasians (8% versus 13%).[4] When they do get feedback, they're unclear about how to act on it, particularly if they were born outside the United States. (See figure 4.) This is a serious problem for corporations that need local expertise to expand their influence in global markets.

In short, because feedback is either absent, overly vague, or contradictory, executive presence remains an inscrutable set of rules for professionals of color—rules they're judged by but cannot interpret and embody except at considerable cost to their authenticity. Consequently, in a workplace where unconscious bias continues to permeate the corridors of power and leadership is mostly white and male, professionals of color are measurably disadvantaged in their efforts to be perceived as leaders.

FIGURE 4

Unclear on how to correct issues raised by feedback

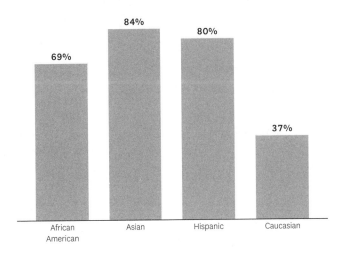

Source: Center for Talent Innovation

As America becomes more diverse at home and its companies are increasingly engaged in the global marketplace, winning in today's fiercely competitive economy requires a diverse workforce that "matches the market." Such individuals are better attuned to the unmet needs of consumers or clients like themselves. Research from CTI shows, however, that their insights need a key ingredient to reach full-scale implementation: a cadre of equally diverse leaders.[5] Yet the power of difference is missing at the top, just when it matters most.

SYLVIA ANN HEWLETT is the founder and CEO of the Center for Talent Innovation and the founder of Hewlett Consulting Partners LLC.

Notes

1. U.S. Equal Employment Opportunity Commission, *Job Patterns For Minorities And Women In Private Industry* (2009 EEO-1 National Aggregate Report), 2009.
2. DiversityInc. staff, "Where's the Diversity in *Fortune* 500 CEOs?" October 8, 2012, https://www.diversityinc.com/diversity-facts/wheres-the-diversity-in-fortune-500-ceos/.
3. S. Hewlett et al., "Cracking the Code: Executive Presence and Multicultural Professionals," Center for Talent Innovation, 2013.

4. S. Hewlett et al., "Vaulting the Color Bar: How Sponsorship Levers Multicultural Professionals into Leadership," Center for Talent Innovation, 2012.
5. S. Hewlett et al., "Innovation, Diversity, and Market Growth," Center for Talent Innovation, 2013.

Adapted from content posted on hbr.org,
January 22, 2014 (product #H00MV0).

6

For a Corporate Apology to Work, the CEO Should Look Sad

By Sarah Green Carmichael

S traight up, we made some mistakes," Whole Foods co-CEOs John Mackey and Walter Robb said in a video apology in response to an over-charging scandal.

"We weren't prepared for the crisis, and we dropped the ball," wrote Airbnb CEO Brian Chesky on the Airbnb blog in 2011, after a guest trashed a host's home.

"This should never have happened. It is simply unacceptable," said Mary Barra, CEO of GM, in one of several public apologies in the wake of safety scandals at the automaker.

The corporate apology, once a relative rarity, has become a normal part of business discourse. Stuff happens, and then we say we're sorry for it. But just because corporate apologies have become commonplace doesn't mean they're all created equal.

Two new studies shed light on what makes some apologies effective and what makes others backfire.

First, Leanne ten Brinke of the UC Berkeley Haas School of Business and Gabrielle S. Adams of the London Business School examine how expressions of emotion affect corporate apologies. Publishing in the journal *Organizational Behavior and Human Decision Processes*, they present the findings of two studies.[1]

In the first study, they looked at how investors reacted to real apologies from executives. They examined 29 online videos of apologies made between 2007 and 2011. Using an established system for distinguishing facial expressions (the Facial Action Coding System, or FACS), their researchers watched each video second by second, without sound, and tracked the expressions that flitted across the executives' faces. Were they frowning? Smiling? Looking sad? Then Brinke and Adams looked at what happened to the company's stock price after the apology. They found that for those leaders who had apologized with a smile, the stock price dropped—perhaps because the leader seemed insincere delivering his apology, or even seemed to be enjoying the suffering his company had caused. The more the person smiled, the worse his company performed.

For the leaders who appeared genuinely contrite, at first it seemed like there was no impact on stock price: The company neither performed worse nor performed better. "Normative emotions simply allow the company to move forward," they write.

But then the researchers took a closer look at CEO apologies, specifically—16 out of the 29 cases. They found that when an apology was delivered by a CEO who looked sad, the company's stock price actually rose post-apology. They determined that "a good apology can build investor confidence," especially in the long term.

To investigate this further, Brinke and Adams conducted an experiment in which they hired an actor to portray an airline CEO apologizing for a computer malfunction that canceled 140 flights, stranding thousands of passengers—a scenario based on a real Alaska Airlines snafu. They made sure his fictional apology contained all the verbal elements of a good apology: the components previous research has identified as being central to repairing relationships, including an explicit "I'm sorry," an offer of repair, an explanation, taking responsibility, and a promise of forbearance. They then recruited subjects to watch this fictional CEO apologize—either happily, sadly, or neutrally. When the CEO appeared sad, participants rated him as more sincere and were more likely to want to reconcile with him. When the CEO delivered his apology with a smile on his face—or, interestingly, a neutral expression—the study participants were less likely to trust him, and the apology even seemed to exacerbate their negative feelings.

Even seasoned leaders are likely to find delivering an apology to be an uncomfortable experience, and when we feel uncomfortable, a normal reaction is to grimace, laugh awkwardly, or even try to break the tension with a joke. Leaders (especially Americans) may also feel they can't show too much sadness or anguish but instead must present a positive front at all times. The research by Brinke and Adams reminds us how these understandable impulses can backfire.

Another paper that appeared in the *Journal of Corporate Finance* adds an interesting wrinkle to this subject.[2] Researchers Don Chance, James Cicon, and Stephen P. Ferris examined 150 press releases from 1993 to 2009 to examine how companies fared when they blamed themselves for poor performance as opposed to blaming external factors. They found that while companies are twice as likely to blame external factors when things go wrong, passing the buck results in continued financial decline. Conversely, companies that take responsibility for their missed earnings stabilize and eventually see an uptick in financial performance. (Interestingly, both groups were about equally likely to fire their CEOs.)

Why? After eliminating numerous factors, the researchers conclude that being honest and specific about the source of the problem—both characteristics of self-blaming statements—not only cheers up investors, it likely helps the company turn around the issue more quickly. Conversely, the companies that blamed external factors were often vague (blaming "economic forces" for instance) and seen as less honest (since many of their wounds had actually been self-inflicted).

The message is loud and clear: When you mess up, admit it. And look appropriately sad about it.

SARAH GREEN CARMICHAEL is a senior editor at *Harvard Business Review*. Follow her on Twitter @skgreen.

Notes

1. L. ten Brinke and G. Adams, "Saving Face? When Emotion Displays During Public Apologies Mitigate Damage to Organizational Performance," *Organizational Behavior and Human Decision Processes* 130 (2015): 1–12.
2. D. Chance, J. Cicon, and S. Ferris, "Poor Performance and the Value of Corporate Honesty," *Journal of Corporate Finance* 33 (2015): 1–18.

Adapted from "Research: For a Corporate Apology
to Work, the CEO Should Look Sad," hbr.org,
August 24, 2015 (product #H02AMD).

7

Are Leaders Getting Too Emotional?

An interview with Gautam Mukunda
and Gianpiero Petriglieri by Adi Ignatius
and Sarah Green Carmichael

There's a lot of crying and shouting both in politics and at the office. Gautam Mukunda of Harvard Business School and Gianpiero Petriglieri of INSEAD help us try to make sense of it all.

Sarah Green Carmichael: *It seems today, with leaders being in public more, there is an emphasis on our leaders always being authentic—that's the buzzword. And tears and shouting do seem to exude authenticity. Gianpiero, what do you make of that? Are our leaders crying and shouting to prove to us that they are real in some way?*

Gianpiero Petriglieri: I don't think people care about leaders being authentic. I think people care about leaders being consistent. Emotions are a great way to convey that you mean what you're saying.

I think we also need to make a distinction between people in positions of power, where emotional expression is always problematic because you expect a certain contained demeanor—although norms are changing, as Gautam has said—and leaders, where emotions are the whole thing. Emotions constitute the connection between people whom we follow and ourselves. So just because you happen to be in a position of visible power, that doesn't mean people regard you as a leader.

In fact, demonstrating emotion is a way of claiming, "Hey, I'm here. I think you should pay attention to this. And I am credibly voicing a concern that we should all care about." Emotions are a way in which people in power try to lead.

Adi Ignatius: *Gianpiero, let me follow up on that because you said that people don't care about their leaders being authentic, and that's basically challenging an entire industry—a sub-industry in the management business that says leaders do need to be authentic. Talk about that a little bit, particularly in the context of emotions. You almost sounded Machiavellian in what you were saying, that a leader can be whatever—they can be emotional—but the point is to be consistent and therefore effective. Can you talk more about that?*

GP: Now when you talk about authenticity, you're talking about two different things. One is spontaneity, which is to say, "I voice my feelings of the moment." Now that might—or much more likely might not—be appropriate for you as a leader.

Then, another part of authenticity means, "I voice credibly, consistently, and authentically the feelings that other people are also feeling. I am showing that we are, in a way, sharing the same concern. I am, in many ways, concerned and I care about the same things that you care about."

This is what you see leaders doing all the time. Sometimes in a Machiavellian way. But sometimes in a very genuine way. In fact, one of the very reasons why we end up following someone is because they seem to be genuinely concerned about things we care about. In politics you see it a lot. You see in political campaigns one candidate saying, "I am one of you guys. I am like you. I have your same background. I care about the same things. But this other guy, he or she is really out for themselves." And the other person is saying the same thing: "No, no, no. *I'm* actually talking about what we all care about. And this other person is out for themselves."

Whoever manages to define themselves as one of us and define the opponent as personally interested wins. So what I'm saying is we don't particularly care that our leader is expressing something that's authentic to them. What we really care about is that our leader is expressing emotions that are meaningful to us.

This is why emotional expression is a double-edged sword. Because sometimes people interpret an emotion as essentially an act of selfishness— that the emotion is really an expression of you being more preoccupied with yourself than with me.

But sometimes people interpret an emotion as an act of generosity: This really shows that you were feeling what I am also feeling. Remember Bill Clinton? In '92 there was a moment during his first campaign where he said in a rally, "I feel your pain." And that remained a legendary moment in his first election. Because he was doing what leaders always try to do, not always manipulatively or in a way that's Machiavellian, but often very genuinely to convey that the leader shares not just the same *understanding* of our situation but the same *experience* of our situation. This is what most of us have always wanted in the people that we then trust to lead, not just that they intellectually understand our circumstances, but that they feel what it's like to be in our circumstances—that they feel our pain, they feel our concerns, they aspire to our same aspirations, they desire our same desires.

That's ultimately what we care about when we say we want leaders to be authentic. We want them to have a lived understanding of our predicament. We don't just want them to express what happens to be true to them at that particular moment.

AI: *Gautam, do you agree with that? Because that seems to be a statement that empathy and emotional intelligence are really the key to leadership. I'm simplifying, but does that all make sense to you?*

Gautam Mukunda: I think empathy and emotional intelligence are extraordinarily powerful keys to leadership. You do often hear people saying—if you look at the Trump phenomenon here in the United States, for example—that they want leaders to tell them what they really think, as opposed to just telling them what the leader *thinks* they want to hear in order to gain power.

But of course it's worth noting that the same people who say this then support those who tell them what they want to hear, not in fact what they really think. So there is some level of doublethink, where, "Donald Trump says what I think, so that must be what he really thinks."

It's that ability to tell people what they want to hear in a way that they believe that you're being sincere that strikes me as being a pretty effective tool in getting power. And certainly, what I got from Gianpiero's comment is the extent to which we want our leaders to be not just self-interested but interested in the welfare of the group, of the people they lead, as much as themselves. And that, essentially, many of these contests for power involve people struggling to define their opponents as only being self-interested.

I think that's true across almost any organization. A leader who is self-interested is one whose followers will be much less likely to lead. But to me, then, you get this question: What are emotions?

Even a very skilled actor, for example, finds it difficult to fake tears on cue. That's something that even professional actors can struggle with. So when President Obama cries over children who are murdered in a school, there is a sense that he's revealing some deeply held emotion.

It is also striking, of course, that so much of the conservative response to that statement was to suggest that he had onions or something under the podium that were allowing him to fake it, both because I think the people saying this realize how powerful it was to see a president break down in tears and because it reveals something about themselves—that they felt that the murder of many innocent children was somehow something that wouldn't move a person to tears.

GP: You see, I don't think people just want to hear leaders tell them what they think. I think people want to see leaders show them what they themselves feel. They want to see their leaders express the feeling that they also sense to be true.

Of course, not everyone shares the same feelings. The example Gautam brings up—President Obama crying—it's an extremely powerful message. And it humanizes a leader. For people who share the same dismay, the same discomfort, that humanization actually enhances his leadership. And for people who oppose his understanding of the situation, for people who don't share his sentiments, that humanization diminishes his leadership. This is where emotional expression is always a double-edged sword. Because the people who share the sentiments you are expressing will actually feel closer to you and, therefore, feel that you are more of a leader. And the people who don't share those sentiments will suddenly feel more distant from you, and they will suspect that you are being manipulative, Machiavellian, and whatnot.

In that moment, you have a man who occupies one of the most powerful positions of leadership in the world facing, on his watch, a tragedy. A tragedy that, despite all his power, he cannot reverse. He is therefore expressing frustration at the limitation of that power—a frustration that's not just his own but is also expressed on behalf of a large group of people who probably feel that it is a tragedy that could easily have been prevented with political will, with political action. And it isn't prevented simply because there is not enough political will to implement the changes that you would need for gun control.

SGC: *In that moment, President Obama crying—would that moment have been different if he were a female president? Is there something different about when you see a man break down that way and a female leader of that stature break down that way?*

GM: I mean, surely, without a doubt. The criticism that someone is too emotional is one of the classic gendered tropes that are used to go after female leaders. It's worth noting that when Hillary Clinton cried a little bit in 2008 in New Hampshire it was highlighted as one of the high points of her campaign. This was one of the moments that turned it around and put her back into the race against Obama in 2008.

But it's illustrative that one of the criticisms of Hillary is that she's robotic. Right? So that was a breakthrough of that facade.

I think for most women leaders it's a much riskier proposition to cry than for a male leader to do so. It just plays into gendered stereotypes that opponents of that leader can use to weaken them very rapidly.

SGC: *We should also probably mention here that there may be racial stereotypes. There may be other emotions, like maybe anger, that Obama might get in trouble for expressing that Hillary would not.*

GM: Without a doubt. On those few occasions when Barack Obama has revealed how he thinks about the way he presents himself—and it's clear that he is someone who thinks deeply about this kind of thing and is very self-reflective on these issues—he has said that, above all else, the thing that he most strives to avoid is being perceived as the angry black man. That's the phrase that he used. And that this is a profound force that is shaping how he wants to be seen.

He essentially feels that visible expressions of anger are, because of racial dynamics in the United States, almost entirely off limits to him as a leader. And in fact, if you note, before he was reelected, anger was in fact entirely off limits to him as a leader. I can't think of any time that he expressed anger in those first four years. What we've started to see after he was reelected, and particularly in the past year, is that he essentially has more freedom to express these emotions. And he is taking advantage of it quite powerfully on some occasions.

AI: *So given what you said, would you advise female executives to hold their emotions in check? That it may not be fair, but society will still hold it against them if they cry in public in front of their teams?*

GM: First, I would advise any leader, male or female, to work pretty hard to do that. The power of these moments is at least in part precisely because they are rare.

John Boehner's tendency to break down in tears became a punch line in Washington. I don't think it was an asset to his leadership. When Barack Obama did it, it was striking because we had never seen a president do something like that, that I can recall.

So male or female, I would say, if you are extraordinarily emotional at all times, that is likely to be a handicap for you as a leader at least to some extent. I would tell female executives that it is deeply unfair, but they are being judged more harshly.

And they surely know that better than I ever could; I've never spoken with a woman leader who wasn't well aware of that fact and who hadn't thought through the fact that they were being judged by standards that their male counterparts were not.

But it is too easy to use gendered attacks—to argue that someone is overly emotional and not thinking things through—against a female leader, or any female leader in a contentious situation where there are people trying to undercut her, to not be extremely cautious of that concern.

SGC: *Gianpiero, do you have anything to add either about the anger issue or the weeping issue?*

GP: I generally think outrage is a lot easier to fake than sadness. And perhaps a lot easier to mistrust, frankly. See, I think we risk spending too much tension under the stereotypes about what you should or shouldn't do.

I would tend to agree that, especially for a senior or a visible leader in politics or business, it's a good rule of thumb to have a relatively contained demeanor. I also think that anyone who wants to really be a leader—not just call themselves one—

has to have some kind of relationship with their emotional life. They ought to be able to ask themselves not just, "Do I express emotions or not?" but to be a little bit more sophisticated with themselves and with others to ask, "How do I express emotions?"

If you are attentive to the undercurrent of organizational lives, emotions are constantly being expressed. When I work with senior management teams, my first question is never, "Do you openly express emotions or not?" My first question is, "How do you tend to express emotions?"

So, for example, one classic way to scream your divergence with a group's opinion is simply not to show up. Or to show up late to a meeting and say nothing when everyone else is very animated. That's a very overt, very visible expression of disappointment or even aggression. Now, whether that's discussed, whether that's decoded, whether that's verbalized is a different thing. Just because we aren't verbalizing our emotions or melting into tears doesn't mean we aren't expressing strong emotions or that we aren't expressing emotions appropriately. Too detached of an emotional response can very often be extremely inappropriate and extremely ineffective.

So I think, as a leader, the more important questions are: Do you know what you're feeling? And do you know whose feelings those are? Do you know why you're feeling that way? Are you interpreting those feelings just as an expression of your emotional state of the moment? Or are you able to think more deeply about what those feelings are telling you about what's happening around you—what's happening to the people that you're responsible for? And can you make sense of and then articulate them in a way that is useful, in a way that actually advances the task?

GAUTAM MUKUNDA is an assistant professor in the Organizational Behavior Unit of Harvard Business School. He received his Ph.D. from MIT in political science. His first book is *Indispensable: When Leaders Really Matter* (Harvard Business Review Press, 2012). GIANPIERO PETRIGLIERI is an associate professor of organizational behavior at INSEAD, where he directs the Management Acceleration Programme, the school's flagship executive program for emerging leaders. A medical doctor and psychiatrist by training, he researches and practices leadership development. Follow him on Twitter @gpetriglieri. ADI IGNATIUS is the editor in chief of *Harvard Business Review*. SARAH GREEN CARMICHAEL is a senior editor at *Harvard Business Review*. Follow her on Twitter @skgreen.

Adapted from "Are Leaders Getting Too Emotional?" on *HBR IdeaCast* (podcast), March 17, 2016.

Index

Invaluable insights
always at your fingertips

With an All-Access subscription to
Harvard Business Review, you'll get
so much more than a magazine.

Exclusive online content and tools
you can put to use today

My Library, your personal workspace for sharing,
saving, and organizing HBR.org articles and tools

Unlimited access to more than 4,000 articles in the
Harvard Business Review archive

Subscribe today at hbr.org/subnow

The most important management ideas all in one place.

We hope you enjoyed this book from *Harvard Business Review*. For the best ideas HBR has to offer turn to HBR's 10 Must Reads Boxed Set. From books on leadership and strategy to managing yourself and others, this 6-book collection delivers articles on the most essential business topics to help you succeed.

HBR's 10 Must Reads Series

The definitive collection of ideas and best practices on our most sought-after topics from the best minds in business.

- Change Management
- Collaboration
- Communication
- Emotional Intelligence
- Innovation
- Leadership
- Making Smart Decisions

- Managing Across Cultures
- Managing People
- Managing Yourself
- Strategic Marketing
- Strategy
- Teams
- The Essentials

hbr.org/mustreads

Buy for your team, clients, or event.
Visit hbr.org/bulksales for quantity discount rates.